# AUTUMN
## —AND—
# WINTER

*Seasoned by God*

M ESHELLE  B ROWN

authorHOUSE®

*AuthorHouse™*
*1663 Liberty Drive*
*Bloomington, IN 47403*
*www.authorhouse.com*
*Phone: 1 (800) 839-8640*

*Published by AuthorHouse 08/10/2016*

*ISBN: 978-1-5246-2039-4 (sc)*
*ISBN: 978-1-5246-2037-0 (hc)*
*ISBN: 978-1-5246-2038-7 (e)*

*Library of Congress Control Number: 2016911957*

*Print information available on the last page.*

*Any people depicted in stock imagery provided by Thinkstock are models, and such images are being used for illustrative purposes only. Certain stock imagery © Thinkstock.*

*This book is printed on acid-free paper.*

# DEDICATION

I dedicate this book to my family sister-jean brown, Brothers'- Thomas and Ken Brown, God, and to all of the readers who love my book.

Meshelle Brown

# CONTENTS

# WINTER

# ACKNOWLEDGEMENT

I thank Authorhouse publishing. And God. For none of this would be possible without them.

# AUTUMN

# Autumn Actually

Autumn actually is a second spring
But solitarily fall is prettier looking
Oft' leaves show an indian summer
All laying on the ground till winter
Fog lingerith round orange pumpkin
Faded emerald grass acold crispyfill
That garnering moon is breathtaking
Thus arising high over elohim's hill
Three painted hills verily in bounds
Thence gigantic' riparian floated low
Nine colored trees stand out around
Not that far from apond's edge flow
Cometh gray smoke from a chimeny
Floated towards an ivorial palen sky
There woodman's ax sticks into tree
Abides' in yard beside house nearby
Blessed' father agave indian summer
Falling leaves should aseason it best
Occurred before an ivory white winter
Plus puttin' steamy summer into rest

By: Meshelle Brown

# Autumn Afternoon

Now in front yard one autumn afternoon
Leaves laying everywhere a leafy' strewn
Is one squirrel standin' underneath a tree
Then climbing fast within a chestnut tree
Thus' going from branch to branch quick
Chestnut falls straight down from the tree
Aptly dropping like a thin miniature stick
Chestnuts lays thence all over the ground
Babby squirrel nibbling on a nut it found
Within the neighbor's yard from next door
And upon gods tender warm day to adore
Nine black birds and babies are astanding
Within the back yard walking and looking
And baby squirrel's tummy is full of nuts
Sets in tree on branch sees them chestnuts
The people under tree pickin' up chestnuts
None will be 'over looked nor shall forget
Picking em' and dropping em' into bucket
Now proud to have a nutless clean ground
of this very same time' all the year round


By: Meshelle Brown

# AUTUMN COLORED MOUNTAIN

God made an autumn colored mountain
Filled with so many various fused trees
Seen over and over apt' distantly again
Cherry-red' yellow-gold' and green trees
The mountain has assorted hueful colors
Elohim painted it various blushed stains
Far away all pretty suffused in splendor
So ampling are these mixed color stains
God's masterpiece is the gigantic' world
Distant colors 'all sewed in grassy green
Blue sky and white clouds within world
He touches' on every hilltop in between
Plus' large valleys that sets down below
He's also added a sunbeam to set aglow
'Yellow sunshine' everywhere to and fro
Breezy 'barely' blowing then getting still
Brown bird in tree on branch sitting still
Within the world high in mountains' hill
Therein autumn's colored' mountain style
To keenly see far away drawing' a smile

By: Meshelle Brown

# Autumn Cometh Along

Autumn cometh along every year
Upon them hillsides far and near
The trees turning to red and gold
Yet' yellows are those marrigolds
A gentle hush spreads on thereby
At close range on field so serene
Whited clouds drift in a blue sky
Ton' of buttercups to the extreme
In integral field of golden brown
The autumn grown' harvest tis in
A ripe garden is picked on down
Cooketh also preserving food again
A bluish haze on the distant hills
Wild geese are in southward flight
Sunsets hueish deep purplish hills
Fall' skies harvest moon is bright
Autumn's the only prettiest season
That willeth forever be very grand
Of god's awesome' autumn season
In which he smiles upon earthland

By: Meshelle Brown

# Autumn Day Textured

God's autumn day is leafy textured
The falling leaves all tumble down
Whetheral meaning a furly surfaced
To bless a good grassfilled' ground
God's wind blowing leaves to flow
All around to empty cornfield rows
Then bronze-tipped pheasants go fly
'Advancing towards white cloud sky
The ripe apples hang from the tree
Reflects sun mellowy days carefree
Golden pears hang in orchard trees
Lookin' beautiful within them trees
Ten large' pumpkins in garden patch
A huge brown field holds haystacks
Leaves layin' on pumpkins in patch
Beside also 'around' them in abatch
A tall tree upon first branch at best
Looking up at straw-made bird nest
Young babies then raise their heads
With opened beaks ready to be fed
Come on home dearest mother bird
To a leaf-fill'd autumn day textured

By: Meshelle Brown

# Autumn Day

Autumn day first one begins today
'Bronze leaf dropping verily today
Thereon a dim green ground it lay
Oft' yonder shadow hillside of old
Sun in sky a beaming yellow gold
Upward within a sky sun's in hold
The fall' maple tree god had made
All leaves fall like feather' brigade
Fat ripe' apples upon orchard trees
Ready' to be pulled off of the tree
Flyin along seventeen bees humbly
Sits on flower sips nectar thirstinly
Amany woodland trail birches shine
All deep green tones etch on pines
Around tree flows a green ivy vine
Squirrel hides acorn into the ground
By the oak tree within leafy ground
Falls' harvest proves bountiful yield
Within dirt rich soil gardening field
It distantly looketh very good today
For god makes a warm autumn day

By: Meshelle Brown

# Autumn Days

Several passing autumn days are beautiful
With only one red leafed' tree is plentiful
And in the front yard looking all ablazed
The 'bright' red color leaves very amazed
Thousands lay there alas looking so pretty
By an early mornin' their wet and sweaty
Air drying them off by middle of the day
Next yard is full maple trees stand in way
With some green pine trees that too stand
Withal it's needles attached there on hand
Still onto the branches of tree in leafland
Small 'black and white' dog in back yard
'Walking around in leaves with self-regard
Enjoying what is left of a warm fall' day
Before 'cooly temperatures come this way
Summer falters on while fall begins today
When lots of leaves lay upon that ground
And moreover a pumpkin patch an around
It is time for god to give summer a boot
So miss autumn can periodically take root

By: Meshelle Brown

# AUTUMN EXPLOSION

An 'autumn explosion arrived with leaves
Which 'covereth the front also back yards
Five trees are still half-way full of leaves
Thence' more leaves will fall in the yards
Until there is no more leaves in the trees
Their changing from leafy to barren' trees
Hillish' bank topped in pretty purple thrift
Miniature lavendar flowers' lord god's gift
The big' large red leaves mostly shine out
Fromal the yella' leaves around also about
Leaves alain' over dim green grass on top
All rabbits in posterior' yard enjoy hip-hop
In fallen leaves of god's dew-filled ground
Squirrels pick-up eat pecans on wet ground
Thus' the yards are full of nuts also leaves
The ground tis loaded in millions of leaves
Three to four colors sometimes more color
Alas' evermore just one single fitting color
As northwinds blow shaking the trees bare.
Causing a autumn explosion grounds' ware

By: Meshelle Brown

# AUTUMN FUNFAIR

Autumn funfair likely midst the daylight

Autumn leaves go falling in earth's light

Whethersoever amany places far and near

A charming' carnival of colors look dear

Leaves is 'whirling around on the ground

'Whimfully falling little by little in bound

Just laying still in the yard after they fell

Wee miniature creatures play in em' well

Looking so sweet walking through leaves

Kids carefully hold them in air with ease

Lovin' to be held within autumn's funfair

Puppies standin by tree in textured leaves

Elohims day timedly flows on by like air

The even' is here and campfire is burning

Setting around to boot in a circling' style

Along with several friends to kindly smile

Holding marshmellows onto stick aroasting

All of them alooking nicely golden brown

This fantastic fall day tis closing on down

Making this night seem really worth while

Withal leaves here as the coldness appears

Means the lord gives an extra special mile

Telling all that winter is ever coming near

By: Meshelle Brown

# Autumn Harvest

Awesome autumn harvest had come again.
Long blossomin' rectangle garden contains
The fallen colored leaves do yearly appear
On the cocoa dirt ground around and near
Making ground look all brownfully stained
Seeds was asown when spring had reigned
Then one fine day 'twas all harvest grown
Furthermore elohims rain drop on it's own
Thereal the men came picking harvest bare
The fruits and vegetables all went elsewhere
Now cook and can put into jars for winter
Then set them on shelves in storage shelter
Until the fallwinter time openin' one to eat
During cold season enjoy a pint sized treat
Them autumn trees not far from the garden
Looking full glossed and stands at attention
Thence shedding it's leafless form tho' later
Now that this food garden is totally austere
Furthermore all wholly bare at it's very best
Thanks blessed god for fall' autumn harvest

By: Meshelle Brown

# Autumn Is At It's Best

Autumn is at it's best when blazed
Withal it's colors a bright and bold
Seen flowers far away also 'amazed
Thematic' treasures of a purest gold
An all maxed' out field the prettiest
And in garden were orange pumpkins
Them ivory corn ears is the 'whitest
All yellow corn ears is also their kin
Still in 'teal green silk shuck around
Attach'd to stalk into the dirt ground
God's sun shines within the blue sky
As sun rays nourish the earth thereby
Along with vegetables food gardeness
Alas yella' daisies field of maxedness
Also is two separate fields a few feet
Distant of each other looking so neat
Is garden and maxed field both pretty
But arnaxed' field is even more pretty
Of dear god's seasonal' treasure chest
A blazing scene autumn is at it's best

By: Meshelle Brown

# Autumn Is Coming

Autumn is coming from god to all
The wind induces the leaves to fall
Alain' there upon the tranquil trails
Later Mr. winter will come to avail
'Since slow swaying wind will dote
It is blowing all these leaves afloat
Coursing through those auburn hills
Amoving forward of their own will
Winter is near autumn's fallen chill
Continuing on course' of god's will
Most trees do go barend and bereft
Some keep 'pretty in autumnic cleft
In an appealing emerald green gloss
It fades into a dimmish green gloss
Limbs sway in autumn's wild wind
'Some shed in a early winter's tend
Leaves 'fall off into a timed release
Averily dropping the last few leaves
Quarterly autumn carries on it's cue
Then the winter season begins anew

By: Meshelle Brown

# Autumn Is Prettiest

Autumn is 'prettiest because of them trees
Astanding into exterior and posterior yards
Those tall plush blazing also flaming trees
Surely does beautify the whole entire yard
Withal their leaves laying upon the ground
Looking ever so lovely all yards in bound
Autumn is prettiest upon face of mountain
Blazin flaming trees are all over mountain
Which is looking 'truly beautiful from afar
Cause god brought old 'fallen Autumn ajar
Various colors 'prettier than shade of green
Though beautiful as a flurried ivorial scene
Autumn 'tis prettiest with flamed leaf hills
Fromal' distance it's a splendid cutest spill
The pretty painted yards in along the street
Looketh dazzlin all over a real scenic treat
Autumn is pretty hence totaled on all earth
The nature trail often fillst of golden mirth
Multiple color over one hue looks the best
God gave autumn and it looks the prettiest

By: Meshelle Brown

# AUTUMN MIST

An early fog grayish chiffon autumn mist
Often sweetly flowing alas heaven kissed
Fairly fallin' blush that dawn cannot hide
Copperd sunset streaked with yellow gold
The softened sonnets whispers by the tide
And god's changing hand is there to hold
A second springed weather upon the earth
Still railroad train in sterling parallel lines
Goes forward through autumn misted birth
Them living flowers within yard look fine
The placid eggwhite fog o' quiet little feet
Stayed there in atmosphere to kindly greet
All peoples dogs cats birds hearts do beat
Like second hand on watch ticking a beat
Theatrical twilight are asteeped in perfume
Smell of trickled honeysuckle upon a wall
Through woodland lushed of 'lacing plume
However adappled moonlight softly do fall
Overt world that's stretching far plus wide
Elohims hand severed seasons to subdivide
Spring sununer autumn winter timely abide

By: Meshelle Brown

# Autumn Morn

Dawn is arrived the first autumn morn
With meager leaves pecans plus acorns
Close to road within the posterior yard
Leaves also lay behind in exterior yard
All upon ground around the maple tree
Stand heart leaf asters plus white lilies
Maxed around tree edged in red bricks
Standing along side by side is redbrick
Surrounding the flowers and in a circle
Butterflies roaming around likely aflittle
Within warming rays of the golden sun
Bumble bees begin feasting one by one
On a sweet liquid from tangerine mum
Alas' sitting short time on orange mum
Then ahoppin' scotch onto the next one
Grim crickets sit in wet dewfilled grass
Chirping awhile within the 'robust mass
God's chalky albino clouds adrift on by
Few chocolate birds often fly in the sky
Of a mid morn greeting the autumn sky


By: Meshelle Brown

# Autumn Season Yard

Autumn seasoned yard lined in apples of gold
And bedecked with red apples bright and bold
Also layeth green granny' apples which is cute
All are levied' around tree to the side to boot
Whereas them wild grape vines are tightly tied
Alas those pigeon birds is looking all pie-eyed
Standing there at a vine twisted barbwire fence
Withal the multiple colored' apples in sequence
A front yard has long row of brick blue sumac
Of self-same line likely' is alabaster white lilac
Corresponding tis' sassafras of which looks fair
Oscillating wind shaketh them necked plus bare
During that latteral fall season preceding winter
Furthermore weather often god seasonal changer
Which is how we get fromal' autumn to winter
Yearly first part of autumn is an indian summer
Quarterly in fall the ground is variously colored
A yellow gold crimson red beige brown colored
Then fall is warm then 'twill turn to quick cool
Finally cold last ten days winter comes on ajule

By: Meshelle Brown

# AUTUMN SPLENDOR HUES

Those autumn splendor hues are fully in swing
Looking pretty on them branches there in cling
Crimson plus amber also gold leaves often fall
Withal' help from the wind that comes to call
Ever so constant it's an annual thrilling delight
Behold all magic colors of autumn's even light
Them rustling leaves are apted lovable lullabies
Join to 'thematic warmth of these autumn skies
Imbuing overal a light blue as nature conceives
The pleasantness of an autumn weather receives
As distant harvestful moon reflecting once more
Am bountiful wealth coming from heaven's store
Those beautiful blooms of the warm summer lie
Faintly whispers to autumn a farewell good bye
All o' flaming pizzazz of summer season at last
'Twill linger a while then fade on into the past
Thematic' treasures upon earth do solitarily find
Them autumn splendor hues it's elohim's design
Looks awesome everyone who sees it each year
Very pretty and beautiful day after day per year

By: Meshelle Brown

# Autumn Time

Autumn time leaves are falling now
Slowly floatin' their way down now
Coverin' with a blanket onto ground
Messy all over looking 'leafy bound
Like pieces of a huge jigsaw puzzle
Horses eat the straw without muzzle
Positioned looking downward at hay
God's light blue sky is turning gray
Frost lingers around orange pumpkin
Sittin' on porch oh country bumpkin
Within a huge yard for amany miles
There's orange jack o' lantern smiles
And so their face glow to amuse us
A grinning and entirely beguiling us
An stringy straw all over the ground
With candied apples into baskets too
Looking pretty sitting on hay mound
And mums of every fall colored hue
With eleven gourds in assorted sizes
Lookin' beautiful when the sun rises
At 'autumn time god made surprises

By: Meshelle Brown

# Autumn Will Fall

Faithfully' the autumn will fall
For god above dwells over all
The warblers shall stay awhile
'Until that cold comes in style
Then they eat food in autumn
After the scarecrow scares 'em
They won't be back till spring
All multiple' leaves are falling
Into two yards and on the hill
Dropping' fromalt trees at will
The trees 'pretty all mountains
Amany beautiful colored stains
From a distance' at a roadside
Grand view farer mountainside
A brown yellowy gold crimson
Hues that captivate 'fall season
Birds trees leaves upon ground
Tis best part same time around
'Per year elohim comes to call
So his autumn season will fall

By: Meshelle Brown

# Autumn Winter Spring Summer

Autumn winter spring summer
Will appear in our midst later
On the horizon will be bright
God continues within the light
Then four season' befall to us
When o autumn vanishes thus
Winter will come in it's place
Melting off is snowhite's face
All of them people smile adu
The spring rebirth is next too
An emerald greens all we got
The summer is warm also hot
'Hot makes people homebound
Autumn tree leave's somewhat
Cover the earths' good ground
Fall temps' is warm cool cold
Winter cold and 'freezing cold
Some winter days is warmfold
Four seasons are always adorn
Of god's subdued an earthborn

By: Meshelle Brown

# Autumn Is Welcomed

Autumn is welcomed after mid September
Now them pine trees wear indian summer
Dresses of emerald and furthermore umber
With lord's sky above in soft silky shawl
Of gray and silver superior booting to all
And wind leaving a aromatic' spicy scent
Then atraveling in way summer had went
Tho' the warm autumn arrives here today
Thus' taking over in a distant small town
Them blackbirds squall winging their way
'Home in flight on ample fields of brown
Hazed silver wood smoke flowing around
Also floating upward from the dry leaves
Next autumn befalls with a tinted' brown
On the outskirts of town in such an ease
Beginning' with a multiple-color-reflection
Trees also leaves begin changing direction
Furthermore some fall down into sequence
Meaning half leaves left is fall's evidence
'Autumn' hence welcomed into providence

By: Meshelle Brown

# AUTUMNAL MONTHS

Behold these latter autumnal months
Emerges shortly after mid September
'With the October November months
And ends just before 'solstice winter
The father put 'fall' season on earth
With awesomey phases colorful hues
Indian summer with a 'flaming earth
Emerald bank sewed in purplish hue
Ways off of purple bank thrifted-hill
Of rododendrums built-in ivory frills
Wildly grown in weeds bladed grass
Once in a while rododendrums 'alas
At times stand in a meadow or yard
Happenstance via prairie or any yard
Cherry-red also crimson flamed trees
Four burgundy bush maple leaf trees
Make yard look pretty distantly away
As do all mountains o' farther away
Flamed colors pretty a earth all over
Of autumnal months yearly roll over

By: Meshelle Brown

# WINTER

# WINTER BALL

Winter ball started the eve of christmas
Just a few days preceding the new year
When snowflakes fell in the street 'alas
They swirled and swayed in good cheer
Twirling round' on the east main street
Like lady ballerina's dancing real sweet
They're 'flowing happily through the air
All just a-whirling into the thoroughfare
It's fun watching them snowflurries fall
Lowering into beauty withal god's grace
Noticin in the wind a dropping snowfall
To descend on a streets' navy-white face
All cities upon an earth have winter ball
Upon them streets per every single town
During the beginning oft' black nightfall
Snowflakes comes courtin' in alberttown
Snowleafs will fall into an earliest morn
Though' ending in time for dawn to call
Also receiving this wonderful' day aborn
God gavest christmas an ice white shawl

By: Meshelle Brown

# WINTER BEGINS

Winter begins to step in place
Relieving autumn of his place
As the days get mostly colder
The white snow started to fall
Over the pretty' leaves forever
Others will miss beautiful' fall
Clear ice forms oft' water tide
Chilly north winds mild breeze
Then since humans are outside
Their noses fingers toes freeze
Earth shall sometime be bright
Anthem bells of christmas ring
Dozen' christmas carollers sing
All December skittles' on away
And city people shed' few tear
An ending month and final day
Tonight' last night for this year
Winter begins so then it leaves
With lord's ever changing ease

By: Meshelle Brown

# WINTER DAY MAGIC

Winter day magic in god's world
All the snowflakes persistedly fall
For centuries blanketing the world
A cakey cover that overlays it all
Like a canopy of sparkling white
Within a white sky calm and still
0 clouds overfill the sky in sight
Looking like a cottony ground-fill
That literally is winter day magic
Many trees dressed icily fantastic
Icicled branches look so glazedly
Is delightful for all people to see
No footprints on a mountain lane
To impare it's sweet beauty there
A truly wondrous white fairyland
That all humane look everywhere
All the evergreen's aladend down
Withal snowdrifts along the sides
Oyster white cover autumn brown
As all of humankind likely abides

By: Meshelle Brown

# WINTER DAY

A winter day outside gets chilly
Red cardinal standing near idlely
The emerald holly plus mistletoe
Was frosted within a ivory snow
All youths' went outside to play
Only a little still' on a cold day
They threw snow balls roundelay
At parked cars and people today
From the side on a chillish day
The kids also teens enjoys today
Sleighing while snow was soften
During a beautiful winter season
See icicles attached to roof ledge
Afroze dripping down from edge
Minute per minute droppin along
Fallen icicles melt' now all gone
Snow makes scenery look frosted
God's efforted labor has accosted
An ivorial' white splendor for all
Tis shown on winter day over all

By: Meshelle Brown

# Winter Has Leaves

Winter has leaves from a fall season
Which was a warm cool cold season
Now the leaves laying on the ground
Are idly there 'cause winter's around
Winter has leaves bistered' as can be
Per sole colored depends on the trees
Of name and kind in which it stands
In the ground from the planters hand
That has been around for many years
Because of lord 'I am' rainfalls' tears
Winter has leaves then intact anyway
Never comes undone but stay always
Cause it's mistletoe bush also berries
Red berries abide in bush 'amerrilies'
Stands in ground tall as a roof ledge
Some only high as a window's ledge
Mistle toe leaves long as tree leaves
Aptly are the width of variant leaves
God has gave the seed yielding trees
Winter has leaves that came of trees

By: Meshelle Brown

# WINTER HUE

A winter hue so white everywhere
Feeling the extreme cold bitter air
Daylight appears fully within sight
Beneath ivory sky apt frosty white
Today's wrapped into seasonal hue
No more in rule is brown fall hue
The soft snow is god's gift to you
The red cardinals decorate a scene
On snowwhite boughs of evergreen
The ground is 'lain' in white snow
Polar bear awalks in a plush snow
God presents dark iced snow night
Icy winds do sculpt drifts of white
To sketch each silvery-frosted-night
Winter hue's around day and night
December's holding winter's height
Snow's around few days to a week
Then melts to show a grassy cheek
As during a spell of a winter chill
The new year begins a winter spill

By: Meshelle Brown

# WINTER IS ENRICHED

Winter is enriched with snow and rain
All throughout gods season to entertain
To fall from the sky snowing on earth
To cultivate 'every area' of the ground
Rain dropping often onto bitts of earth
To help nurture the terrain and ground
Snow makes front yards look so lovely
The backside yards lookin' very comely
Then sun shine melts it' abiding awhile
Dries all living things far in many mile
While it's visiting within gods blue sky
Even when the freezing cold is at nigh
And while all of wildlife is hibernating
The human life is busy in warmkeeping
Fromal that outside frozen cold weather
That comes to call from god the father
That stays around for few triad months
So seasons can turn per trio of months
The snow and rain make winter all rich
For acts of god is why winter is enrich


By: Meshelle Brown

# WINTER IS THROUGH

Winter is through on god's time bound
With seven brown 'barren' trees around
Red cheeked' kids riding on their sleds
'Clothed in coats plus boggins on heads
Sixteen children laying within the snow
Movin their arms legs fast within snow
Then once where all the kids had alain
Thus showing many angelic figure stain
Then later on they all had melted away
Within that evening a latter part of day
Thus' the nighttime sky's out to admire
And the moon's there amidst' to inspire
And rudolph's red nose glowing around
In the sky flying into leaps and bounds
Nature is waiting for the creator's hand
To awake from sleep an earth and land
'Apting naturally to a perpetual moment
When barren nature will become instant
Blooming birthful' nature to come anew
Forever after lord's is winter is through

By: Meshelle Brown

# WINTER LEAVES

Winter leaves they layeth upon the ground
Their on front porch and driveway around
Lays within flower pots oft anterior porch
Lays in posterior yard and the back porch
The leaves alay in seats of patio furniture
Often in god's cold twenty degree weather
The ok ground is dressed in a leafy decor
Plus everything else that's outside herefore
Looking at each leafs' front and back face
And know the ground has a leafy' surface
Some begin to crumble in a limited while
But that's part of the winter seasons style
By elohim's wind them leaves are blowed
Around and around within yards unmowed
They have blown aside that house and car
And across into a neighbor's yard so far
All winter leaves raked them into big pile
Stuff them in bags that is very worthwhile
These winter leaves once belongeth to fall
Finally now winter taken it's seasonal call

By: Meshelle Brown

# WINTER NIGHT

Winter night tis vastly cold
Withal stars shining so bold
All of them glow so bright
Even space away and slight
A normal fixed constellation
Of unreached high elevation
Into the lords' midnight sky
Seven homes underneath sky
Sitting on top of the ground
Space 'betwixt them inbound
Smoke flows out of chimney
Fromal indoor firelit chimney
Them trees is empty or bare
Standin in dark without care
Oft' all its roots into ground
Oft' in outer darkness around
Owl' sits onto a first branch
Not far fromst country ranch
Seven horses in the red barn
Two cow two pigs in a barn

By: Meshelle Brown

# WINTER REFLECTION

That winter reflection arrived in white
So ole autumn could fall out of sight
God's snow fell dazzling all aswirling
From a pearly sky soft rapidly falling
Tucking in the world so cold all bare
Asleeping in god's blond blankets fair
Is fathers earth' ground looking pretty
In a soft palen substance like confetti
Also latter fall plus early winter come
The snows presence tis warm welcome
All the beautiful earth shall smile back
When a round sun will shine on track
Even when the slush snow melts away
Plus the chilly wind goeth on it's way
When earth smiles winter day is warm
Even when cool winter day is aswarm
Earth's still smiling when barren again
Oft god's changing hand now and then
Barren season tis dim winter reflection
Also white snow is a winter reflection

By: Meshelle Brown

# WINTER RETURNS

Winter returns to stay for awhile
So the autumn can leave in style
It's left behind the final last leaf
So now mister winter's the chief
The earth's atmosphere to behold
Of a cold winter's shivering fold
Nine black birds stand in a field
Bare empty and no crop in yield
Tho out within the ol' back yard
Where dogs roam of high regard
Tho' the icy chill of mid winter
Exists on earth is froze and icier
Indoor lights shine' in all homes
During the night wild wind roam
Smoke adrifts out of the chimney
Aflowing in dark throughout trees
Elsewhere into bare brown terrain
Tho snowflakes silently fall again
Fromst working hand of god o'er
In land winter returns' once more

By: Meshelle Brown

# Winter Scene

God paints' a winter scene of pearl white
With snow laying onto ground in daylight
An indian summer has been covered over
Withal the snow surrounding a large river
Ice has formed into the small round pond
All children teenagers askate on the pond
To enjoy them selves particularly on today
The parents and kin folks do look in way
While four dogs stand beside their owners
Parting from friends before barking occurs
Hidden away from soft plush snow freeze
Is few brown and black bears with babies
Hibernating sleep until all the snow melts
Birds stay in fromal that winter snow belt
Likely gods winter scene in a white blush
Tho' here it is in place without any brush
T'was made but not put in a picture frame
Per year o winter at times looks the same
Brought on earth by lord's changing hand
Alas all wonderful winter scene dreamland

By: Meshelle Brown

# Winter Snow Fall

A winter snow fall is wonderful
Mesmerized by a white snowfall
The ending snowflurry explosion
It came during a cold summons
That very high hill was covered
Fourteen inch height piled snow
Everywhere it was all ascattered
That green ground even covered
A part of few branches dangling
Tree limbs heavy caked in snow
Making them alook very darling
Entirely loaded in all that snow
Winter begins a few days along
Before year end comes up gone
God warms an atmosphere along
Then all snow melted until gone
Also thence again all looks bare
Sometimes snow's upon the earth
Verily' all caked in splendor fair
Within most parts of god's earth

By: Meshelle Brown

# Winter Snow In The South

When god compels winter at his will
Sometimes snow topples' upon a hill
Scarcely ever falls in the deep south
It solely falls by the "fathers" mouth
Sometimes twill lay for a long while
So all of them southerners will smile
Sometimes it's only here a short time
To melt on off by the afternoon time
How pleasant it is when it does stay
And eating snow cream day after day
Children playin plus having some fun
Making snow man' and snow woman
Dressing them in buttons scarves hats
Give them both a loving little old pat
Thinking their your 'dear' good friend
Before winter comes close' to an end
Here within this 'deep' booming south
Singly amelting by the 'fathers' mouth
Is the winter snow at god's own' will
That the cold interval inclinely' fulfills

By: Meshelle Brown

# Winter Snow

That winter snow tis falling fast
0'er night till day is here at last
A cool pure white 'wooly' mass
Clouds are fluffed brimming alas
The iced snow sent from elohim
Ivory flakes touching the ground
Falling in succession a inch slim
To cover the dully green ground
'Yonder mountain in white snow
Looks wonderful to see at show
Flake after flake made it prized
Upon a cold morn as sun arised
All can enjoy two or three days
Looking at snow white in amaze
Overal because god had breathed
On mountains all yards blanketed
The bushes also look plush white
Them trees look like a icy white
The front yards all a grand show
God gives to all the winter snow

By: Meshelle Brown

# WINTER SNOWFLAKES

Winter snowflakes appear' in the clouds
So they'll look like mighty old trumpets
Just adrifting and moving in the crowd
Snowflakes softly fall forming a blanket
Soon it'll look like a winter wonderland
God clothes various areas of united land
By acovering the ground that is in sight
Small snowflakes begin to spill in might
The cold air made them dancifully swirl
They fell ghostly onto them barren field
Apted to a sheen of singled white pearls
Just falling faster brought' down to yield
Field that formerly looks a necked brown
Along with the trees wears a white gown
That's proceeding on down to green floor
Likely to glisten plus sparkle in splendor
Apt with snowflakes still drifting around
Their all over furthermore an earthbound
Them winter snowflakes really fell down
God's gift to the earth is a white crown

By: Meshelle Brown

# Winter Spring Snow

The winter spring snow hugely' god breathed
Laying on the ground for he had bequeathed
It was piled twelve or more inches in height
Over the 'heart of dixie' in broadest daylight
Which was the result' of a march snowstorm
Just lays on the ground in a soft plush form
White snow is all caked on the tree branches
'Piled in front of mountain like an avalanche
From a far distance mountains look all white
So wonderfully beautiful into an earth's light
Winter spring snow lays all over the rooftops
Of them houses storage buildings and cartops
'Covering all driveways and navy blue streets
Plus the anterior yards and light blue streets
Then birds are in hiding until all snow melts
Falling off the branches within' southern belt
The died out flowers growing back in season
Withal warm temperatures' to be their reason
When snow's leaving and cold becomes cool
Winter spring snow will no longer be in rule

By: Meshelle Brown

# WINTER THE LAST DAY

Winter the last' day had arrived today
A week ago march snow melted away
A grass maxed yard is wholly in sight
Alian far away off from god's skylight
Looking like a short green dimmed dry
Ofal' million blades of grass to behold
Eagle flieth up yonder on high so bold
An shall swoop on down from the sky
Sitting per' rock attached to a mountain
During the moment this year to contain
Of the birds and people who come here
Each passed day into a cold atmosphere
Some insects are within a grass but yet
None will crawl outside in view to get
Because of the winter trees shed leaves
Until they are gone and have no leaves
But very few has leafy dark green look
A few trees have different colored look
Mostly few trees have dark green tinter
Just observing all on last day of winter

By: Meshelle Brown

# Winter Time Schedule

Old man winter has a time schedule
Thus god is that strong creating tool
As the winter frost stipples a picture
Usually on each single window pane
Bare trees stand' a motionless taciturn
Atossed to and fro by wind and rain
A thin moist spreading downy sheen
All a frosty' white instead of a green
God of the season has fit' scheduling
To rest from laboring plans on along
Hibernating until time for cool spring
When them flowers burst out in song
The wintery season has it's own way
To warm up lives with all happiness
Of bringing christmas as a given day
And a nice new year bound to bless
While thematic winter is on the land
Accept it now as a dearly old friend
Awrapping it's arms around all lands
Till spring comes and is warm again

By: Meshelle Brown

# WINTER TREES

Winter trees are coated with god's snow
Dropping down from his blue sky so-so
A huge' snow storm seldom ever comes
When it falls there shall be all welcomes
After that largest white rapid snow storm
It will lay around into softened ice form
On many individual branches to and froe
They'll get so heavy and dangle real low
Sometime snow branches won't hang low
They just extend out looking ivory caked
Standing up like eve' white holliday trees
Lonesome christmas pines are all adecked
In Lord's finest snow that all people sees
Tis' when all winter trees look their best
And not to mention they're most prettiest
Overal' better looking than any other time
Ofal' which they've ever been seen before
Of a ivory snow covered ground evermore
Many snow caked pine tree is most galore.


By: Meshelle Brown

# WINTER WHITE DAY

Winter white day lord gave to all
Awake time seeing snow over all
The acts of god made snow yield
To lay all over a barren dirt field
Besides the wisp wind is blowing
Moreover the snowflakes is falling
Among all hills houses and woods
Elohim god saw that all was good
A raccoon walks in barren' garden
Makin foot prints into snow often
Before a white snow starts to melt
Here within all southern bama belt
Children shall play outside in snow
Or stay inside away from the snow
Far as if adults stand in front door
Watchin' their kids play even more
Buildin snow man or snow woman
Then puttin hats scarves and button
Upon the frosty' couple team today
Thanks god for a winter white day

By: Meshelle Brown

# WINTER WHITE

Winter white is all over the ground
Fell down everywhere laying astrow
In every yard each street all around
It is the extra largest thickest snow
Piled fourteen to twenty inches high
Lord let it drop down from the sky
Fast forming a snowflurry explosion
Starting with a chilly cold summons
Given many inches of ampled' snow
Icy-caked branches are dangling low
Because of stiff snow stuck to them
Layin' on the ground underneath em'
Looking like god's wondrous miracle
Into this last fourth season is special
To all the small girls and boys alike
Standing within a front yard suchlike
While' squirrels asleep in hibernation
Hiding from the white snow duration
Due to the process of weatherization
That father gave to his earthly nation

By: Meshelle Brown

# Winter Wonderland

Often was a land of winter white
Behold forrest is dressed in white
Woe all looks so wonderfly swell
Soft featherd' snowflakes had fell
Across miniature' wooden bridge
Footprints show' all over a bridge
Where someone has traipsed today
Moreover 'lord' was around today
After bridge footprints also afflame
Alas were all over the nearest hill
Quite a few grey rabbits had came
To stop and sniff of the snowspill
Standin there looking at snowprint
Within god's wondrous white flint
Them rabbits 'scampered' on away
Upon thin snow in their own way
Father's working hand is a delight
To give to all a morning of white
American forrest a handsome land
Oft' spectacular winter wonderland

By: Meshelle Brown

# WINTER MORNING LIGHT

Winter morning light 'began' by dawn
Behind the house tis woods plus fawn
God sent 'iced' snow to visit everyone
'Especially' to the children one by one
His snow is a special gift that's adorn
To be covered overt the beautiful land
Hence in particular in amidst the morn
Oftentimes looked at by those on hand
All theatrical winter white that's ashorn
Tho' now overal hear that joyous noise
'Quite' a many of them girls plus boys
Playing into ivorial fluffed' fallen snow
Seven children build a mister snowman
There along beside him is snow woman
They are both frosty husband wife team
Apt' hats buttons scarves to an extreme
Sitting therein the iced' soft ivory snow
Looking verily sweet moreover beautiful
Even more cute than red christmas bow
Winter morning light it's forever special

By: Meshelle Brown

Printed in the United States
By Bookmasters